Advice She Actually Wants

MESSAGES FOR THE PREGNANT NEW MOM
FROM LOVED ONES

MELISSA PENNEL

Follow Your Fire Publishing
Sacramento, CA

Melissa Pennel / Follow Your Fire Publishing
FollowYourFireCoaching.com
Sacramento, CA.

Ordering Information:
Quantity sales: Special discounts are available on quantity purchases by corporations, associations, and others. For details, contact the publisher at the address above.

Advice She Actually Wants: Messages for the Pregnant New Mom from Loved Ones—1st ed.

Paperback ISBN: 978-1-956446-17-3
Hardback ISBN: 978-1-956446-18-0

This journal is not a substitute for professional counseling or mental health services. Please contact an organization below or one local to you for more support. Also see page 117 for pregnancy and postpartum mental health resources.

www.nami.org
www.postpartum.net

This journal belongs to

_____

Due date

_____

If found please contact

_____

More Journals by the Author

The Questions You'll Wish You Asked:
A Time Capsule Journal Series

After losing my mom before asking her important questions, I created
a journal to write down stories, wisdom, and advice for my children.
There's now a journal for every family relationship.

A Time Capsule Journal for Mothers & Daughters

A Time Capsule Journal for Mothers & Sons

A Time Capsule Journal for Fathers & Daughters

A Time Capsule Journal for Fathers & Sons

A Time Capsule Journal for Parents & Children

A Time Capsule Journal for Grandfathers

A Time Capsule Journal for Grandmothers

A Time Capsule Journal for Grandparents

A Time Capsule Journal for Treasured Mentors
and Important Relationships

Write down answers for your kids.
Ask questions of your elders. Your future self will thank you.

•——————•

The Motherless New Mother's Pregnancy Journal: Prompts, Practices,
and Affirmations to Guide the Mom Who Is Missing Her Own

•——————•

The Book Lover's Companion: Personal Reading Log,
Book Review Prompt Journal, and Book Club Guide

The Book Lover's Companion for Teens

The Book Lover's Companion for Kids

•——————•

Learn more at:
FollowYourFireCoaching.com

CONTENTS

To all mothers, but especially those wondering if they're up to this task.
You are.

A NOTE TO MOTHERS
(& THOSE WHO LOVE THEM)

The journey to motherhood is a big deal.

Pregnancy is a rollercoaster of overwhelming physical changes, wildly fluctuating emotions, and the realization that at some point there will be a tiny human to keep alive. Early motherhood is a mix of the most joy and the most terror ever felt in the same body, all while a woman's eyes, boobs, and undercarriage are leaking her very insides right out.

She's probably wearing a diaper to boot. It's a lot.

Add to the mix those clickbait articles scrolling by, the momstagram highlight reels on social media, and the strangers who give her well-intentioned (but unsolicited) advice, and this poor new mama can start to wonder how in the hell she's actually gonna pull this off.

Enter "The Advice She Actually Wants" journal: a collection of heartfelt words, laughs, and the reassurance that only a new mom's actual community can give. It's basically a bonfire of heartfelt wisdom in a book that she can open when she most needs it.

The journal begins with short prompts for guests at the baby shower/mother's ceremony to fill in; this mix of brief silly and serious questions allow those gathered a chance to celebrate the new mom, make some guesses about the baby, and create a fun keepsake for her to page through later.

The section that follows, Wisdom From Other Moms, is a space for longer messages from the "seasoned" moms in her life. These prompts take a little more time and reflection, and include questions to elicit advice, cheer the new mama on, and ideas for how she can resource strength when drowning in the early days of motherhood. The Wisdom From Other Moms prompts can be filled in privately by each advice-giver, serve as the inspiration for one on one conversations, or act as topics within a women's circle or mother's blessing.

The journal wraps with a space for mama to jot down her own reflections, record the gifts she's been given, and concludes with some mantras to give her fuel and sustenance. There's also a section for professional mental health resources to access during pregnancy and postpartum - because it is always okay to seek additional support.

Together, these sections form a sisterly circle of protection from the anxiety, uncertainty, and overwhelm so common in early motherhood. Because yes, becoming a mother is a lot to take on - but with a community surrounding her, supporting her, and reminding her how to access her own inner-badassery, this new mama will be totally up to the challenge.

With love and sisterly solidarity,
Melissa Pennel

Shower Notes

for Mama & Baby

MESSAGES

Why I know you'll be a great mom:

When you're overwhelmed, remember the time that you:
(other tough thing mama has accomplished)

Other messages to remind you of your amazing-ness:

PREDICTIONS

Baby's birth date:

Baby's birth weight:

lbs   oz

Eye Color:

Hair Color:

Baby will inherit:

From Mom: From Dad:

Why this baby is lucky to have you as parents:

My Promise:

I _____Name_____ , commit to being a part of your support and holding you up on the tough days. I will check in with you, show up with coffee/chocolate/hugs/memes, support you whether you're crying or laughing, and help you to know that you're loved, supported, and never alone on this journey.

MESSAGES

Why I know you'll be a great mom:

....

....

....

When you're overwhelmed, remember the time that you:
(other tough thing mama has accomplished)

....

....

....

....

....

Other messages to remind you of your amazing-ness:

....

....

....

....

....

....

....

....

PREDICTIONS

Baby's birth date:

Baby's birth weight:

lbs   oz

Eye Color:

Hair Color:

Baby will inherit:

From Mom: From Dad:

Why this baby is lucky to have you as parents:

My Promise:

I _____ Name _____ , commit to being a part of your support and holding you up on the tough days. I will check in with you, show up with coffee/chocolate/hugs/memes, support you whether you're crying or laughing, and help you to know that you're loved, supported, and never alone on this journey.

MESSAGES

Why I know you'll be a great mom:

When you're overwhelmed, remember the time that you:
(other tough thing mama has accomplished)

Other messages to remind you of your amazing-ness:

PREDICTIONS

Baby's birth date:

Baby's birth weight:

lbs   oz

Eye Color:

Hair Color:

Baby will inherit:

From Mom: From Dad:

Why this baby is lucky to have you as parents:

My Promise:

I _____Name_____ , commit to being a part of your support and holding you up on the tough days. I will check in with you, show up with coffee/chocolate/hugs/memes, support you whether you're crying or laughing, and help you to know that you're loved, supported, and never alone on this journey.

MESSAGES

Why I know you'll be a great mom:

When you're overwhelmed, remember the time that you:
(other tough thing mama has accomplished)

Other messages to remind you of your amazing-ness:

PREDICTIONS

Baby's birth date:

Baby's birth weight:

lbs   oz

Eye Color:

Hair Color:

Baby will inherit:

From Mom: From Dad:

Why this baby is lucky to have you as parents:

My Promise:

I _____Name_____ , commit to being a part
of your support and holding you up on the tough
days. I will check in with you, show up with coffee/
chocolate/hugs/memes, support you whether you're
crying or laughing, and help you to know that you're
loved, supported, and never alone on this journey.

MESSAGES

Why I know you'll be a great mom:

When you're overwhelmed, remember the time that you:
(other tough thing mama has accomplished)

Other messages to remind you of your amazing-ness:

PREDICTIONS

Baby's birth date: Baby's birth weight:

                                                    lbs   oz

Eye Color: Hair Color:

Baby will inherit:

From Mom: From Dad:

Why this baby is lucky to have you as parents:

My Promise:

I _____ Name _____ , commit to being a part of your support and holding you up on the tough days. I will check in with you, show up with coffee/chocolate/hugs/memes, support you whether you're crying or laughing, and help you to know that you're loved, supported, and never alone on this journey.

MESSAGES

Why I know you'll be a great mom:

When you're overwhelmed, remember the time that you:
(other tough thing mama has accomplished)

Other messages to remind you of your amazing-ness:

PREDICTIONS

Baby's birth date: Baby's birth weight:

                                                    lbs   oz

Eye Color: Hair Color:

Baby will inherit:

From Mom: From Dad:

Why this baby is lucky to have you as parents:

My Promise:

I _____ Name _____ , commit to being a part of your support and holding you up on the tough days. I will check in with you, show up with coffee/chocolate/hugs/memes, support you whether you're crying or laughing, and help you to know that you're loved, supported, and never alone on this journey.

MESSAGES

Why I know you'll be a great mom:

When you're overwhelmed, remember the time that you:
(other tough thing mama has accomplished)

Other messages to remind you of your amazing-ness:

PREDICTIONS

Baby's birth date: Baby's birth weight:

                                  lbs   oz

Eye Color: Hair Color:

Baby will inherit:

From Mom: From Dad:

Why this baby is lucky to have you as parents:

My Promise:

I _____Name_____ , commit to being a part of your support and holding you up on the tough days. I will check in with you, show up with coffee/chocolate/hugs/memes, support you whether you're crying or laughing, and help you to know that you're loved, supported, and never alone on this journey.

MESSAGES

Why I know you'll be a great mom:

When you're overwhelmed, remember the time that you:
(other tough thing mama has accomplished)

Other messages to remind you of your amazing-ness:

PREDICTIONS

Baby's birth date:

Baby's birth weight:

lbs   oz

Eye Color:

Hair Color:

Baby will inherit:

From Mom: From Dad:

Why this baby is lucky to have you as parents:

My Promise:

I _____ Name _____ , commit to being a part of your support and holding you up on the tough days. I will check in with you, show up with coffee/ chocolate/hugs/memes, support you whether you're crying or laughing, and help you to know that you're loved, supported, and never alone on this journey.

Why I know you'll be a great mom:

When you're overwhelmed, remember the time that you:
(other tough thing mama has accomplished)

Other messages to remind you of your amazing-ness:

PREDICTIONS

Baby's birth date: Baby's birth weight:

                                              lbs   oz

Eye Color: Hair Color:

Baby will inherit:

From Mom: From Dad:

Why this baby is lucky to have you as parents:

My Promise:

I _____ Name _____ , commit to being a part of your support and holding you up on the tough days. I will check in with you, show up with coffee/chocolate/hugs/memes, support you whether you're crying or laughing, and help you to know that you're loved, supported, and never alone on this journey.

MESSAGES

Why I know you'll be a great mom:

When you're overwhelmed, remember the time that you:
(other tough thing mama has accomplished)

Other messages to remind you of your amazing-ness:

PREDICTIONS

Baby's birth date:

Baby's birth weight:

lbs   oz

Eye Color:

Hair Color:

Baby will inherit:

From Mom: From Dad:

Why this baby is lucky to have you as parents:

My Promise:

I _____ Name _____ , commit to being a part of your support and holding you up on the tough days. I will check in with you, show up with coffee/chocolate/hugs/memes, support you whether you're crying or laughing, and help you to know that you're loved, supported, and never alone on this journey.

MESSAGES

Why I know you'll be a great mom:

When you're overwhelmed, remember the time that you:
(other tough thing mama has accomplished)

Other messages to remind you of your amazing-ness:

PREDICTIONS

Baby's birth date: Baby's birth weight:

                                                    lbs   oz

Eye Color: Hair Color:

Baby will inherit:

From Mom: From Dad:

Why this baby is lucky to have you as parents:

My Promise:

I _____ Name _____ , commit to being a part of your support and holding you up on the tough days. I will check in with you, show up with coffee/chocolate/hugs/memes, support you whether you're crying or laughing, and help you to know that you're loved, supported, and never alone on this journey.

MESSAGES

Why I know you'll be a great mom:

When you're overwhelmed, remember the time that you:
(other tough thing mama has accomplished)

Other messages to remind you of your amazing-ness:

PREDICTIONS

Baby's birth date: Baby's birth weight:

                                                    lbs   oz

Eye Color: Hair Color:

Baby will inherit:

From Mom: From Dad:

Why this baby is lucky to have you as parents:

My Promise:

I _____Name_____ , commit to being a part of your support and holding you up on the tough days. I will check in with you, show up with coffee/chocolate/hugs/memes, support you whether you're crying or laughing, and help you to know that you're loved, supported, and never alone on this journey.

MESSAGES

Why I know you'll be a great mom:

When you're overwhelmed, remember the time that you:
(other tough thing mama has accomplished)

Other messages to remind you of your amazing-ness:

PREDICTIONS

Baby's birth date:

Baby's birth weight:

lbs   oz

Eye Color:

Hair Color:

Baby will inherit:

From Mom:

From Dad:

Why this baby is lucky to have you as parents:

My Promise:

I _____ Name _____ , commit to being a part of your support and holding you up on the tough days. I will check in with you, show up with coffee/chocolate/hugs/memes, support you whether you're crying or laughing, and help you to know that you're loved, supported, and never alone on this journey.

MESSAGES

Why I know you'll be a great mom:

When you're overwhelmed, remember the time that you:
(other tough thing mama has accomplished)

Other messages to remind you of your amazing-ness:

PREDICTIONS

Baby's birth date: Baby's birth weight:

                                      lbs   oz

Eye Color: Hair Color:

Baby will inherit:

From Mom: From Dad:

Why this baby is lucky to have you as parents:

My Promise:

I _____ Name _____ , commit to being a part of your support and holding you up on the tough days. I will check in with you, show up with coffee/chocolate/hugs/memes, support you whether you're crying or laughing, and help you to know that you're loved, supported, and never alone on this journey.

MESSAGES

Why I know you'll be a great mom:

When you're overwhelmed, remember the time that you:
(other tough thing mama has accomplished)

Other messages to remind you of your amazing-ness:

PREDICTIONS

Baby's birth date: Baby's birth weight:

                                          lbs   oz

Eye Color: Hair Color:

Baby will inherit:

From Mom: From Dad:

Why this baby is lucky to have you as parents:

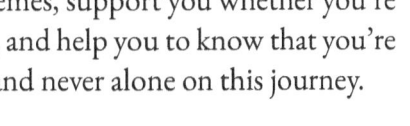

My Promise:

I _____ Name _____ , commit to being a part of your support and holding you up on the tough days. I will check in with you, show up with coffee/chocolate/hugs/memes, support you whether you're crying or laughing, and help you to know that you're loved, supported, and never alone on this journey.

MESSAGES

Why I know you'll be a great mom:

When you're overwhelmed, remember the time that you:
(other tough thing mama has accomplished)

Other messages to remind you of your amazing-ness:

PREDICTIONS

Baby's birth date: Baby's birth weight:

                                                    lbs   oz

Eye Color: Hair Color:

Baby will inherit:

From Mom: From Dad:

Why this baby is lucky to have you as parents:

My Promise:

I _____Name_____ , commit to being a part of your support and holding you up on the tough days. I will check in with you, show up with coffee/chocolate/hugs/memes, support you whether you're crying or laughing, and help you to know that you're loved, supported, and never alone on this journey.

MESSAGES

Why I know you'll be a great mom:

When you're overwhelmed, remember the time that you:
(other tough thing mama has accomplished)

Other messages to remind you of your amazing-ness:

PREDICTIONS

Baby's birth date: Baby's birth weight:

                                      lbs   oz

Eye Color: Hair Color:

Baby will inherit:

From Mom: From Dad:

Why this baby is lucky to have you as parents:

My Promise:

I _____ Name _____ , commit to being a part of your support and holding you up on the tough days. I will check in with you, show up with coffee/chocolate/hugs/memes, support you whether you're crying or laughing, and help you to know that you're loved, supported, and never alone on this journey.

MESSAGES

Why I know you'll be a great mom:

When you're overwhelmed, remember the time that you:
(other tough thing mama has accomplished)

Other messages to remind you of your amazing-ness:

PREDICTIONS

Baby's birth date: Baby's birth weight:

                                            lbs   oz

Eye Color: Hair Color:

Baby will inherit:

From Mom: From Dad:

Why this baby is lucky to have you as parents:

My Promise:

I _____Name_____ , commit to being a part of your support and holding you up on the tough days. I will check in with you, show up with coffee/chocolate/hugs/memes, support you whether you're crying or laughing, and help you to know that you're loved, supported, and never alone on this journey.

MESSAGES

Why I know you'll be a great mom:

When you're overwhelmed, remember the time that you:
(other tough thing mama has accomplished)

Other messages to remind you of your amazing-ness:

PREDICTIONS

Baby's birth date: Baby's birth weight:

                                            lbs   oz

Eye Color: Hair Color:

Baby will inherit:

From Mom: From Dad:

Why this baby is lucky to have you as parents:

My Promise:

I _____ Name _____ , commit to being a part of your support and holding you up on the tough days. I will check in with you, show up with coffee/chocolate/hugs/memes, support you whether you're crying or laughing, and help you to know that you're loved, supported, and never alone on this journey.

MESSAGES

Why I know you'll be a great mom:

When you're overwhelmed, remember the time that you:
(other tough thing mama has accomplished)

Other messages to remind you of your amazing-ness:

PREDICTIONS

Baby's birth date:

Baby's birth weight:

lbs   oz

Eye Color:

Hair Color:

Baby will inherit:

From Mom: From Dad:

Why this baby is lucky to have you as parents:

My Promise:

I _____ Name _____ , commit to being a part of your support and holding you up on the tough days. I will check in with you, show up with coffee/chocolate/hugs/memes, support you whether you're crying or laughing, and help you to know that you're loved, supported, and never alone on this journey.

MESSAGES

Why I know you'll be a great mom:

When you're overwhelmed, remember the time that you:
(other tough thing mama has accomplished)

Other messages to remind you of your amazing-ness:

PREDICTIONS

Baby's birth date: Baby's birth weight:

                                               lbs   oz

Eye Color: Hair Color:

Baby will inherit:

From Mom: From Dad:

Why this baby is lucky to have you as parents:

My Promise:

I _____ Name _____ , commit to being a part of your support and holding you up on the tough days. I will check in with you, show up with coffee/chocolate/hugs/memes, support you whether you're crying or laughing, and help you to know that you're loved, supported, and never alone on this journey.

MESSAGES

Why I know you'll be a great mom:

When you're overwhelmed, remember the time that you:
(other tough thing mama has accomplished)

Other messages to remind you of your amazing-ness:

PREDICTIONS

Baby's birth date: Baby's birth weight:

                                            lbs   oz

Eye Color: Hair Color:

Baby will inherit:

From Mom: From Dad:

Why this baby is lucky to have you as parents:

My Promise:

I _____Name_____ , commit to being a part of your support and holding you up on the tough days. I will check in with you, show up with coffee/chocolate/hugs/memes, support you whether you're crying or laughing, and help you to know that you're loved, supported, and never alone on this journey.

MESSAGES

Why I know you'll be a great mom:

....

....

....

When you're overwhelmed, remember the time that you:
(other tough thing mama has accomplished)

....

....

....

....

....

Other messages to remind you of your amazing-ness:

....

....

....

....

....

....

....

PREDICTIONS

Baby's birth date: Baby's birth weight:

                                                    lbs   oz

Eye Color: Hair Color:

Baby will inherit:

From Mom: From Dad:

Why this baby is lucky to have you as parents:

My Promise:

I _____Name_____ , commit to being a part of your support and holding you up on the tough days. I will check in with you, show up with coffee/chocolate/hugs/memes, support you whether you're crying or laughing, and help you to know that you're loved, supported, and never alone on this journey.

MESSAGES

Why I know you'll be a great mom:

When you're overwhelmed, remember the time that you:
(other tough thing mama has accomplished)

Other messages to remind you of your amazing-ness:

PREDICTIONS

Baby's birth date: Baby's birth weight:

                                        lbs   oz

Eye Color: Hair Color:

Baby will inherit:

From Mom: From Dad:

Why this baby is lucky to have you as parents:

My Promise:

I _____Name_____ , commit to being a part of your support and holding you up on the tough days. I will check in with you, show up with coffee/chocolate/hugs/memes, support you whether you're crying or laughing, and help you to know that you're loved, supported, and never alone on this journey.

MESSAGES

Why I know you'll be a great mom:

When you're overwhelmed, remember the time that you:
(other tough thing mama has accomplished)

Other messages to remind you of your amazing-ness:

PREDICTIONS

Baby's birth date:

Baby's birth weight:

lbs   oz

Eye Color:

Hair Color:

Baby will inherit:

From Mom: From Dad:

Why this baby is lucky to have you as parents:

My Promise:

I _____ Name _____ , commit to being a part of your support and holding you up on the tough days. I will check in with you, show up with coffee/chocolate/hugs/memes, support you whether you're crying or laughing, and help you to know that you're loved, supported, and never alone on this journey.

Wisdom from Other Moms

Messages of Love and Sanity

MESSAGES OF LOVE

I am _____Name_____ , daughter of _____Mother's Name_____, granddaughter of
_____Maternal Grandmother's Name_____ .

Something that surprised me about motherhood:

Something to look forward to about motherhood:

When you're feeling anxious or depleted, I suggest:

(AND SANITY)

What I would do differently if I could start over:

Why I know you'll be a great mom:

How I can offer support:

- Grocery shopping
- Checking in via phone calls/ texts/memes
- Bringing coffee/sustenance
- Helping you get poop stains out of pajamas/laundry
- My other ideas:

- Running errands
- Babysitting/babyholding/hand holding
- Providing/arranging meals
- Cleaning your house

I am _____Name_____ , daughter of _____Mother's Name_____, granddaughter of
_____Maternal Grandmother's Name_____ .

Something that surprised me about motherhood:

Something to look forward to about motherhood:

When you're feeling anxious or depleted, I suggest:

What I would do differently if I could start over:

Why I know you'll be a great mom:

How I can offer support:

- Grocery shopping
- Checking in via phone calls/texts/memes
- Bringing coffee/sustenance
- Helping you get poop stains out of pajamas/laundry
- My other ideas:

- Running errands
- Babysitting/babyholding/hand holding
- Providing/arranging meals
- Cleaning your house

I am _____Name_____ , daughter of _____Mother's Name_____, granddaughter of

_____Maternal Grandmother's Name_____ .

Something that surprised me about motherhood:

Something to look forward to about motherhood:

When you're feeling anxious or depleted, I suggest:

(AND SANITY)

What I would do differently if I could start over:

Why I know you'll be a great mom:

How I can offer support:

- Grocery shopping
- Checking in via phone calls/ texts/memes
- Bringing coffee/sustenance
- Helping you get poop stains out of pajamas/laundry
- My other ideas:

- Running errands
- Babysitting/babyholding/hand holding
- Providing/arranging meals
- Cleaning your house

MESSAGES OF LOVE

I am _____Name_____ , daughter of _____Mother's Name_____, granddaughter of
_____Maternal Grandmother's Name_____ .

Something that surprised me about motherhood:

Something to look forward to about motherhood:

When you're feeling anxious or depleted, I suggest:

(AND SANITY)

What I would do differently if I could start over:

Why I know you'll be a great mom:

How I can offer support:

- Grocery shopping
- Checking in via phone calls/ texts/memes
- Bringing coffee/sustenance
- Helping you get poop stains out of pajamas/laundry
- My other ideas:

- Running errands
- Babysitting/babyholding/hand holding
- Providing/arranging meals
- Cleaning your house

MESSAGES OF LOVE

I am _____Name_____ , daughter of ___Mother's Name___, granddaughter of
___Maternal Grandmother's Name___ .

Something that surprised me about motherhood:

....

....

....

....

Something to look forward to about motherhood:

....

....

....

....

When you're feeling anxious or depleted, I suggest:

....

(AND SANITY)

What I would do differently if I could start over:

Why I know you'll be a great mom:

How I can offer support:

- Grocery shopping
- Checking in via phone calls/ texts/memes
- Bringing coffee/sustenance
- Helping you get poop stains out of pajamas/laundry
- My other ideas:

- Running errands
- Babysitting/babyholding/hand holding
- Providing/arranging meals
- Cleaning your house

I am _____Name_____ , daughter of ___Mother's Name___, granddaughter of
_____Maternal Grandmother's Name_____ .

Something that surprised me about motherhood:

Something to look forward to about motherhood:

When you're feeling anxious or depleted, I suggest:

(AND SANITY)

What I would do differently if I could start over:

Why I know you'll be a great mom:

How I can offer support:

- Grocery shopping
- Checking in via phone calls/ texts/memes
- Bringing coffee/sustenance
- Helping you get poop stains out of pajamas/laundry
- My other ideas:

- Running errands
- Babysitting/babyholding/hand holding
- Providing/arranging meals
- Cleaning your house

MESSAGES OF LOVE

I am _____Name_____ , daughter of ____Mother's Name____, granddaughter of

____Maternal Grandmother's Name____ .

Something that surprised me about motherhood:

Something to look forward to about motherhood:

When you're feeling anxious or depleted, I suggest:

(AND SANITY)

What I would do differently if I could start over:

Why I know you'll be a great mom:

How I can offer support:

- Grocery shopping
- Checking in via phone calls/ texts/memes
- Bringing coffee/sustenance
- Helping you get poop stains out of pajamas/laundry
- My other ideas:

- Running errands
- Babysitting/babyholding/hand holding
- Providing/arranging meals
- Cleaning your house

MESSAGES OF LOVE

I am _____Name_____ , daughter of ____Mother's Name____, granddaughter of
____Maternal Grandmother's Name____ .

Something that surprised me about motherhood:

Something to look forward to about motherhood:

When you're feeling anxious or depleted, I suggest:

(AND SANITY)

What I would do differently if I could start over:

Why I know you'll be a great mom:

How I can offer support:

- Grocery shopping
- Checking in via phone calls/ texts/memes
- Bringing coffee/sustenance
- Helping you get poop stains out of pajamas/laundry
- My other ideas:

- Running errands
- Babysitting/babyholding/hand holding
- Providing/arranging meals
- Cleaning your house

MESSAGES OF LOVE

I am _____Name_____ , daughter of ___Mother's Name___, granddaughter of
___Maternal Grandmother's Name___ .

Something that surprised me about motherhood:

_____

_____

_____

_____

_____

Something to look forward to about motherhood:

_____

_____

_____

_____

_____

When you're feeling anxious or depleted, I suggest:

_____

_____

_____

_____

(AND SANITY)

What I would do differently if I could start over:

Why I know you'll be a great mom:

How I can offer support:

- Grocery shopping
- Checking in via phone calls/ texts/memes
- Bringing coffee/sustenance
- Helping you get poop stains out of pajamas/laundry
- My other ideas:

- Running errands
- Babysitting/babyholding/hand holding
- Providing/arranging meals
- Cleaning your house

I am _____Name_____ , daughter of _____Mother's Name_____, granddaughter of
_____Maternal Grandmother's Name_____ .

Something that surprised me about motherhood:

Something to look forward to about motherhood:

When you're feeling anxious or depleted, I suggest:

What I would do differently if I could start over:

Why I know you'll be a great mom:

How I can offer support:

- Grocery shopping
- Checking in via phone calls/ texts/memes
- Bringing coffee/sustenance
- Helping you get poop stains out of pajamas/laundry
- My other ideas:

- Running errands
- Babysitting/babyholding/hand holding
- Providing/arranging meals
- Cleaning your house

I am _____Name_____ , daughter of _____Mother's Name_____, granddaughter of
_____Maternal Grandmother's Name_____ .

Something that surprised me about motherhood:

....

....

....

....

Something to look forward to about motherhood:

....

....

....

....

When you're feeling anxious or depleted, I suggest:

....

....

....

....

What I would do differently if I could start over:

Why I know you'll be a great mom:

How I can offer support:

- Grocery shopping
- Checking in via phone calls/texts/memes
- Bringing coffee/sustenance
- Helping you get poop stains out of pajamas/laundry
- My other ideas:

- Running errands
- Babysitting/babyholding/hand holding
- Providing/arranging meals
- Cleaning your house

I am _____Name_____ , daughter of _____Mother's Name_____, granddaughter of
_____Maternal Grandmother's Name_____ .

Something that surprised me about motherhood:

....

....

....

....

Something to look forward to about motherhood:

....

....

....

....

When you're feeling anxious or depleted, I suggest:

....

....

....

....

(AND SANITY)

What I would do differently if I could start over:

Why I know you'll be a great mom:

How I can offer support:

- Grocery shopping
- Checking in via phone calls/ texts/memes
- Bringing coffee/sustenance
- Helping you get poop stains out of pajamas/laundry
- My other ideas:

- Running errands
- Babysitting/babyholding/hand holding
- Providing/arranging meals
- Cleaning your house

I am _____Name_____ , daughter of _____Mother's Name_____, granddaughter of

___Maternal Grandmother's Name___ .

Something that surprised me about motherhood:

_____

_____

_____

_____

Something to look forward to about motherhood:

_____

_____

_____

_____

When you're feeling anxious or depleted, I suggest:

_____

What I would do differently if I could start over:

Why I know you'll be a great mom:

How I can offer support:

- Grocery shopping
- Checking in via phone calls/ texts/memes
- Bringing coffee/sustenance
- Helping you get poop stains out of pajamas/laundry
- My other ideas:

- Running errands
- Babysitting/babyholding/hand holding
- Providing/arranging meals
- Cleaning your house

MESSAGES OF LOVE

I am _____ Name _____ , daughter of _____ Mother's Name _____, granddaughter of
_____ Maternal Grandmother's Name _____ .

Something that surprised me about motherhood:

_____

_____

_____

_____

Something to look forward to about motherhood:

_____

_____

_____

_____

When you're feeling anxious or depleted, I suggest:

_____

_____

_____

_____

What I would do differently if I could start over:

Why I know you'll be a great mom:

How I can offer support:

- Grocery shopping
- Checking in via phone calls/ texts/memes
- Bringing coffee/sustenance
- Helping you get poop stains out of pajamas/laundry
- My other ideas:

- Running errands
- Babysitting/babyholding/hand holding
- Providing/arranging meals
- Cleaning your house

I am _____Name_____ , daughter of ___Mother's Name___, granddaughter of ___Maternal Grandmother's Name___ .

Something that surprised me about motherhood:

Something to look forward to about motherhood:

When you're feeling anxious or depleted, I suggest:

(AND SANITY)

What I would do differently if I could start over:

Why I know you'll be a great mom:

How I can offer support:

- Grocery shopping
- Checking in via phone calls/texts/memes
- Bringing coffee/sustenance
- Helping you get poop stains out of pajamas/laundry
- My other ideas:

- Running errands
- Babysitting/babyholding/hand holding
- Providing/arranging meals
- Cleaning your house

I am _____Name_____ , daughter of _____Mother's Name_____, granddaughter of
_____Maternal Grandmother's Name_____ .

Something that surprised me about motherhood:

Something to look forward to about motherhood:

When you're feeling anxious or depleted, I suggest:

What I would do differently if I could start over:

Why I know you'll be a great mom:

How I can offer support:

- Grocery shopping
- Checking in via phone calls/ texts/memes
- Bringing coffee/sustenance
- Helping you get poop stains out of pajamas/laundry
- My other ideas:

- Running errands
- Babysitting/babyholding/hand holding
- Providing/arranging meals
- Cleaning your house

MESSAGES OF LOVE

I am _____ Name _____ , daughter of _____ Mother's Name _____, granddaughter of
_____ Maternal Grandmother's Name _____ .

Something that surprised me about motherhood:

_____

_____

_____

_____

_____

Something to look forward to about motherhood:

_____

_____

_____

_____

_____

When you're feeling anxious or depleted, I suggest:

_____

_____

_____

_____

(AND SANITY)

What I would do differently if I could start over:

Why I know you'll be a great mom:

How I can offer support:

- Grocery shopping
- Checking in via phone calls/texts/memes
- Bringing coffee/sustenance
- Helping you get poop stains out of pajamas/laundry
- My other ideas:

- Running errands
- Babysitting/babyholding/hand holding
- Providing/arranging meals
- Cleaning your house

I am _____Name_____ , daughter of _____Mother's Name_____, granddaughter of

_____Maternal Grandmother's Name_____ .

Something that surprised me about motherhood:

Something to look forward to about motherhood:

When you're feeling anxious or depleted, I suggest:

(AND SANITY)

What I would do differently if I could start over:

Why I know you'll be a great mom:

How I can offer support:

- Grocery shopping
- Checking in via phone calls/ texts/memes
- Bringing coffee/sustenance
- Helping you get poop stains out of pajamas/laundry
- My other ideas:

- Running errands
- Babysitting/babyholding/hand holding
- Providing/arranging meals
- Cleaning your house

I am _____Name_____ , daughter of _____Mother's Name_____, granddaughter of

_____Maternal Grandmother's Name_____ .

Something that surprised me about motherhood:

Something to look forward to about motherhood:

When you're feeling anxious or depleted, I suggest:

What I would do differently if I could start over:

Why I know you'll be a great mom:

How I can offer support:

- Grocery shopping
- Checking in via phone calls/ texts/memes
- Bringing coffee/sustenance
- Helping you get poop stains out of pajamas/laundry
- My other ideas:

- Running errands
- Babysitting/babyholding/hand holding
- Providing/arranging meals
- Cleaning your house

MESSAGES OF LOVE

I am _____Name_____ , daughter of _____Mother's Name_____, granddaughter of
_____Maternal Grandmother's Name_____ .

Something that surprised me about motherhood:

Something to look forward to about motherhood:

When you're feeling anxious or depleted, I suggest:

(AND SANITY)

What I would do differently if I could start over:

Why I know you'll be a great mom:

How I can offer support:

- Grocery shopping
- Checking in via phone calls/texts/memes
- Bringing coffee/sustenance
- Helping you get poop stains out of pajamas/laundry
- My other ideas:

- Running errands
- Babysitting/babyholding/hand holding
- Providing/arranging meals
- Cleaning your house

MESSAGES OF LOVE

I am _____Name_____ , daughter of _____Mother's Name_____, granddaughter of

_____Maternal Grandmother's Name_____ .

Something that surprised me about motherhood:

Something to look forward to about motherhood:

When you're feeling anxious or depleted, I suggest:

(AND SANITY)

What I would do differently if I could start over:

Why I know you'll be a great mom:

How I can offer support:

- Grocery shopping
- Checking in via phone calls/ texts/memes
- Bringing coffee/sustenance
- Helping you get poop stains out of pajamas/laundry
- My other ideas:

- Running errands
- Babysitting/babyholding/hand holding
- Providing/arranging meals
- Cleaning your house

I am _____Name_____, daughter of _____Mother's Name_____, granddaughter of

_____Maternal Grandmother's Name_____ .

Something that surprised me about motherhood:

....

....

....

....

....

Something to look forward to about motherhood:

....

....

....

....

When you're feeling anxious or depleted, I suggest:

What I would do differently if I could start over:

Why I know you'll be a great mom:

How I can offer support:

- Grocery shopping
- Checking in via phone calls/ texts/memes
- Bringing coffee/sustenance
- Helping you get poop stains out of pajamas/laundry
- My other ideas:

- Running errands
- Babysitting/babyholding/hand holding
- Providing/arranging meals
- Cleaning your house

I am _____Name_____ , daughter of _____Mother's Name_____, granddaughter of
_____Maternal Grandmother's Name_____ .

Something that surprised me about motherhood:

Something to look forward to about motherhood:

When you're feeling anxious or depleted, I suggest:

(AND SANITY)

What I would do differently if I could start over:

Why I know you'll be a great mom:

How I can offer support:

- Grocery shopping
- Checking in via phone calls/ texts/memes
- Bringing coffee/sustenance
- Helping you get poop stains out of pajamas/laundry
- My other ideas:

- Running errands
- Babysitting/babyholding/hand holding
- Providing/arranging meals
- Cleaning your house

I am _____Name_____ , daughter of ___Mother's Name___, granddaughter of
____Maternal Grandmother's Name____ .

Something that surprised me about motherhood:

Something to look forward to about motherhood:

When you're feeling anxious or depleted, I suggest:

(AND SANITY)

What I would do differently if I could start over:

Why I know you'll be a great mom:

How I can offer support:

- Grocery shopping
- Checking in via phone calls/ texts/memes
- Bringing coffee/sustenance
- Helping you get poop stains out of pajamas/laundry
- My other ideas:

- Running errands
- Babysitting/babyholding/hand holding
- Providing/arranging meals
- Cleaning your house

MESSAGES OF LOVE

I am _____Name_____ , daughter of _____Mother's Name_____, granddaughter of
_____Maternal Grandmother's Name_____ .

Something that surprised me about motherhood:

Something to look forward to about motherhood:

When you're feeling anxious or depleted, I suggest:

What I would do differently if I could start over:

Why I know you'll be a great mom:

How I can offer support:

- Grocery shopping
- Checking in via phone calls/ texts/memes
- Bringing coffee/sustenance
- Helping you get poop stains out of pajamas/laundry
- My other ideas:

- Running errands
- Babysitting/babyholding/hand holding
- Providing/arranging meals
- Cleaning your house

Notes by the
New Mom

Reflections & Intentions

REFLECTIONS

What reflections do you have after reading the wisdom and advice shared by your community?

What themes did you notice in their messages?

INTENTIONS

What are some qualities you already possess that will make you a great mother?

For example: perseverance, compassion, flexibility, humor, wonder, etc.

How can you be compassionate and kind to yourself during pregnancy and early motherhood?

For example: allow myself to ask for help, forgive myself when I fall short of my own expectations, create space to be flexible with my plans, spend more time in prayer/ meditation/self-care, write something kind on my mirror, etc.

INTENTIONS

After reading the wisdom from the other mothers in your life, what are some intentions you'd like to set for the rest of your pregnancy and motherhood journey? It's helpful to affirm these in the present, as if it is already so.

For example:

- I am powerful, strong, and my body knows exactly what to do
- I am patient with myself as I forge this new path
- I know that I am doing the best I can and that is always enough
- I am surrounded and supported by friends, family, and my ancestors

Gift Log

Gift: Given By:

Gift: Given By:

Gift: Given By:

Mama's Affirmations

for Pregnancy & Birth

I accept and love my changing body

I am gentle with myself as I feel emotions rise and fall

I have everything I need to be the exact mother I want to be

I trust my body and my baby

My bump is the exact right size for my baby

I am willing to let go of old identities and make way for the person I am now becoming

I am powerful, brave, and strong

I am doing an amazing job

I am always guided, held, and supported on this path

My baby will find the perfect position for birth

My body was made to give birth

My baby and my body know exactly what to do

My birthing body is magic

Birth is beautiful

Each surge brings my baby closer to me

However birth happens is the right way for baby and me

I know that birth is safe

My mental, spiritual, and physical health are valuable

I am exactly who my baby needs

Taking care of myself is loving to everyone around me

It is safe to disappoint people as I embrace this new version of myself

The right people will love me exactly as I am

It is safe to ask for help

I am gentle with myself as I learn how to mother

My best is always good enough and I am doing my best

I know that everything changes and no one phase will last forever

I am a good mother

I am the best mother for this baby

I am always held and supported

Pregnancy and Postpartum Mental Health Resources

Mental health is always important, but the pregnancy/postpartum period is an especially tender time. There is no shame in accessing tools to support you on this journey. Use the below resources as a starting point to accessing support locally.

You are not alone and there is help.

Postpartum Support International
Website: Postpartum.net
Phone: 1-800-944-4773

SAMHSA
(Substance Abuse and Mental Health Services Administration)
Website: SAMHSA.gov
Phone: 1-800-662-HELP (4357)

NAMI (National Alliance on Mental Illness)
Website: NAMI.org
Phone: 1-800-950-NAMI (6264)

National Suicide Prevention Lifeline
Website: suicidepreventionlifeline.org
Phone: 1-800-273-8255

About the Author

Melissa Pennel is a mother, life coach, and author. She believes in the healing power of words, that everyone is a writer if given the right prompts, and that mothers are literal, genuine, non-metaphoric magic. Yes, you.

She lives in Northern California with her partner, children, and beloved cats.

Find more of Melissa's work at:
FollowYourFireCoaching.com